Stanley and Dimitri, two middle-aged men, have lived together for seventeen years, their deep love for each other allowing them to forgive each other's brief infidelities as well as their more trivial domestic differences. Written in a clear and unpretentious blank verse, *The Stanley Parkers* has the two men speaking directly to the audience about their life together, sharing their story with insight, humour and very obvious affection. Though the story is ultimately a sad one, the overriding impression the audience is left with is of the tenderness and warmth of a happy, unselfish relationship.

NORFOLK LIBRARY AND INFORMATION SERVICE	
SUPPLIER	FRENCH
INVOICE No.	18820
ORDER DATE	16-3-95
COPY No.	

The Stanley Parkers

A play

Geraldine Aron

Samuel French—London
New York-Toronto-Hollywood

© 1995 BY GERALDINE ARON

Rights of Performance by Amateurs are controlled by Samuel French Ltd, 52 Fitzroy Street, London W1P 6JR, and they, or their authorized agents, issue licences to amateurs on payment of a fee. **It is an infringement of the Copyright to give any performance or public reading of the play before the fee has been paid and the licence issued.**

The Royalty Fee indicated below is subject to contract and subject to variation at the sole discretion of Samuel French Ltd.

> Basic fee for each and every
> performance by amateurs   Code E
> in the British Isles

The Professional Rights in this play are controlled by Geraldine Aron, c/o 9 Belsize Grove, London, NW3 4UU

The publication of this play does not imply that it is necessarily available for performance by amateurs or professionals, either in the British Isles or Overseas. Amateurs and professionals considering a production are strongly advised in their own interests to apply to the appropriate agents for consent before starting rehearsals or booking a theatre or hall.

ISBN 0 573 04230 6

Please see page vi for further copyright information

The Stanley Parkers was first performed in 1990, by the Druid Theatre Company in Ireland. **Des Keogh** and **Michael Roberts** were directed by **Garry Hynes**.

COPYRIGHT INFORMATION

(See also page iv)

This play is fully protected under the Copyright Laws of the British Commonwealth of Nations, the United States of America and all countries of the Berne and Universal Copyright Conventions.

All rights including Stage, Motion Picture, Radio, Television, Public Reading, and Translation into Foreign Languages, are strictly reserved.

No part of this publication may lawfully be reproduced in ANY form or by any means — photocopying, typescript, recording (including video-recording), manuscript, electronic, mechanical, or otherwise—or be transmitted or stored in a retrieval system, without prior permission.

Licences for amateur performances are issued subject to the understanding that it shall be made clear in all advertising matter that the audience will witness an amateur performance; that the names of the authors of the plays shall be included on all programmes; and that the integrity of the authors' work will be preserved.

The Royalty Fee is subject to contract and subject to variation at the sole discretion of Samuel French Ltd.

In Theatres or Halls seating Four Hundred or more the fee will be subject to negotiation.

In Territories Overseas the fee quoted above may not apply. A fee will be quoted on application to our local authorized agent, or if there is no such agent, on application to Samuel French Ltd, London.

VIDEO-RECORDING OF AMATEUR PRODUCTIONS

Please note that the copyright laws governing video-recording are extremely complex and that it should not be assumed that any play may be video-recorded for whatever purpose without first obtaining the permission of the appropriate agents. The fact that a play is published by Samuel French Ltd does not indicate that video rights are available or that Samuel French Ltd controls such rights.

CHARACTERS

Stanley Parker
Middle-aged. The ideal actor would be short and solid enough to convey the impression that he is overweight. But this is not imperative—alternative lines are included if the actor playing Stanley is slim. Spectacles can be worn.

Dimitri Papavasilopoulos
(Pronounced *Papa-vas-sill-OH-pooh-luss*)
Also middle-aged, but he has taken very good care of himself and is carefully dressed and well groomed. A Greek; his English is slightly accented. Capable of a little Greek dancing.

The action of the play takes place in a bedroom

Time: the present

Other plays by Geraldine Aron
published by Samuel French Ltd

Bar and Ger
The Donahue Sisters
A Galway Girl
Joggers
Same Old Moon
Olive and Hilary

This edition is dedicated to
Robert Patrick
my favourite playwright
and life-long friend

THE STANLEY PARKERS

There is a spacious double bed on stage, and at a distance from the bed, a small collection of lampshades, some newly made and wrapped in polythene, others awaiting attention. There is also a stacked hi-fi system and some Greek albums, and, near the bed, Dimitri's discarded leather slippers. The most unusual feature of the set is an outrageously ostentatious pair of bedside lamps

The lighting is warm and cosy

Stanley and Dimitri are sitting up in bed. Stanley is L, Dimitri is R. Stanley is under the bedclothes, and wears pyjamas and a red silk kimono-style dressing gown. He has a removable pregnancy-style pillow under his pyjamas, to produce a pot belly

(Avoid the use of a duvet as a bedcover because it is too bulky in the later scenes, when we need to see Stanley's diminished outline clearly defined)

Dimitri, wearing a beige wool polo-neck jumper, well-cut beige slacks and toning socks, is sitting on top of the bedclothes. Both men look extremely comfortable and settled

Dimitri is stitching braid to a small and unusual lampshade, working expertly, but at a leisurely pace. Stanley is clutching a large biscuit tin, from which he carefully selects a biscuit. He crunches it with great relish and enjoyment. Dimitri stops stitch-

ing and slowly turns to give Stanley a withering look. Stanley responds with a cheerful smile and offers the biscuit tin. Dimitri declines with a slow shake of the head

Although Stanley eats many biscuits during the play, he avoids delivering lines with his mouth full

Dimitri Stanley was slim when I met him.
Not handsome, not sexy,
I wouldn't say that.
But Stanley was certainly slim.

Stanley Sometimes I feel Dimitri's eyes on me,
as I'm cleaning my teeth, leaning over the basin.
He looks at my stomach,
which, it has to be said, is inclined
to bulge over my pyjama bottoms. (*He sighs heavily*)
I must make an effort. I really must. (*After dwelling on this for a moment, he dips into the tin again*)

Dimitri As you've probably guessed—(*he presents his profile, with great pride*)
I am Greek.
The usual story,
the poor Island family,
the boy was artistic
got sent to the mainland,
turned into a fairy.
The usual story.

Stanley Dimitri makes lampshades in any material—
tasselled or plain, whatever they want.
We're invited to parties to unveil these artworks,
Dimitri's the star, when the lamps get switched on.
He gets rounds of applause and long thank-you speeches.

	You'd swear it was Christmas in Regent Street!
Dimitri	I make EXquisite lampshades in WONderful fabrics
	for BEAUTiful women with time on their hands.
	If my mother could see how I'm welcomed at parties.
	The clasping of hands and the kissing of cheeks!
	Stanley comes with me, tucks into the food.
Stanley	If Dim had been given an arts education,
	his name would be famous today.
	In décor, or fashion, or fabric design.
	There's no doubt about it,
	he would've been someone.
	Dimitri. (*He smiles impishly*)
	Or Dimwit, as I like to call him.
Dimitri	He has a degree, as he often reminds me,
	the result of his studies in art.
	Most of his friends have the same piece of paper,
	and sometimes—the nerve—they will question my background.
	"Gentlemen," I say, without turning a hair,
	"I have a Ph.D. in lampshades,
	from the University of Enlightenment".
	Stanley works hard in a famous design shop.
	He's a décor consultant
	and sometimes does windows.
	That's how we met,
	when I offered them lampshades.
	Stan offered lunch at a smart place in town.
Stanley	I fancied him straight off,
	though he was a bit scruffy,
	and his hair was in need of a cut and shampoo,
	But something about him was very appealing,
	so I asked him to lunch at the end of our meeting

The Stanley Parkers

Dimitri We had grilled calamari and salad with feta
and I had a chat with a waiter from Poros,
a beautiful boy who got off at three thirty.
While consulting the menu, I called for advice.
Made arrangements to meet him, all spoken in Greek.
While Stanley looked on, with a smile on his face.

Stanley We went to a Greek place and had calamari
and Dim started flirting with one of the waiters.
I once spent two months on the Island of Hydra
and knew enough Greek to make sense of their chitchat—
heard Dimwit arranging to phone him that night.

Dimitri We lunched for three hours,
myself and slim Stanley.
The Greek boy went off with a mime that said "phone me" (*He mimes holding a phone to his ear*)
We talked about lighting and interesting dishes
and somehow I never did phone the young waiter.

Stanley Dim moved into my place the following week,
within hours he'd changed all my lampshades.
Before long it was clear,
we were out of the running,
withdrawn from the market,
a settled-down couple.
We were known as an item: (*he inscribes three words in the air*)
"The Stanley Parkers"

Dimitri I didn't see why, when they made us a pair,
we were known as "The Stanley Parkers".
Why not "The Dimitri Papavasilopoulos's"?
But other than that, I had no reservations.

	We were then in our thirties and tired of the scene,
	(*he looks fondly at Stanley*)
	I was happy to settle with this dear old queen.
Stanley	We've been living together for seventeen years—
	sometimes I just can't believe it.
	Each of us owns half a share in this house.
	A risk, people told me, in our situation.
	But so far so good, no regrets whatsoever.
Dimitri	Sometimes, in revenge for the biscuit crumb bed,
	I sprinkle a little sugar on the floor of the kitchen.
	Stanley goes crazy when he feels it underfoot
	—you'd think he was walking on red hot coals.
	He grabs for the brush
	and sweeps himself breathless—
	muttering like a madman!
Stanley	Dimitri's got a thing about cutlery
	—teaspoons to be exact
	When the dishwasher's emptied,
	Dim likes the teaspoons
	returned to their drawer
	and placed neatly and nesting,
	all facing in one direction (*He releases the biscuit tin long enough to place a hand on his hip, an arm to the side, teapot style*)
	"Oh very dainty, Doris". I say, to annoy him.
	"Are we a dainty piece of rough?"
Dimitri	Considering his background,
	he's amazingly ignorant,
	about the things that really matter.
	A Greek, for example,
	would never yawn in the face of a guest——
Stanley (*using Dimitri's accent*)	—or put a milk bottle out, without rinsing it——

Dimitri   His mother has a maid.
"Big deal," I told him, "my mother IS a maid!"
Stanley   (*checking his reflection in the biscuit tin lid*) My chin has
now doubled and much to my horror,
the salesman in AH-MEN declared I was portly.*
"Forty-Four Portly Short" to add insult to injury.
(*He shakes his head worriedly, then absentmindedly pops a biscuit into his mouth*)
Dimitri   A boy in Stan's showroom, a new boy, Jean-Paul,
developed an interest in Stanley.
Of course he was flattered and had an affair. (*He gives Stanley a murderous look*)
He knows that I know,
but it's never been mentioned.
But now Stanley owes me one—that's understood.
Stanley   Dim went to Greece to visit the old folk,
came back with a love bite, that couldn't be hidden.
A love bite at his age!
No fool like an old one.
But now we are quits and the slate is wiped clean.
Dimitri   Living with Stanley does have its moments:
Such as seeing him dance in his red silk kimono.
He descends the stairs slowly,
one step at a time.**
Forty-four portly short with his little fat legs.

If the actor is slim and/or tall, substitute these lines:

*   … the salesman in AH-MEN declared I had "thickened".
            "Double breasted from now on" to add insult to injury.

**   … one step at at time
            a barrel of fun—on stick insect legs
            he has me in stitches, I laugh till I'm weak.

The Stanley Parkers

	He has me in stitches, I laugh till I'm weak.
Stanley	When Dimitri gets sad, he goes Greek.
	First he sings—and believe me,
	his nibs Demis Roussos
	has no competition.
	Then he dances. With squats, twisted hanky and
	leaping and bounding.
	Later, exhausted, he weeps for his island
	—bless him, he hates it so much when he's there.
	His mum came to see us,
	a widow in black.
	With baskets of foodstuff—not actually livestock—
	but goat's cheese and dried fish
	and lemons and ouzo
	and olives to last us ten years.
Dimitri	My mum knows I'm gay.
	I wrote her a letter before she left Greece.
	She liked Stan at once—an instant rapport.
	But while she was here, I did not share his bedroom.
	We got drunk one evening and all danced together
	and Stan started doing his staircase routine.
	But I wouldn't let him,
	it didn't seem proper.
	I have always respected my mother.
Stanley	Mother arrived
	in a cloud of Chanel.
	Bearing Dom Perignon and a kilo of pâté.
	I told her that we were old buddies,
	from way back—
	said we'd purchased the house
	as a form of investment.
	Early one morning, she caught me returning

from our room to the spare (*he looks a bit bashful*)
with a smile on my face.
"Your investment still sleeping?" she said,
sweeping past me,
and left the same day,
with the coolest of hugs.

Dimitri Didn't like Stanley's mother a bit.
She never stopped talking about his great brother,
not to mention his wife and their
OUTSTAAAANDING children.
She told stories of rich men, seduced for their assets,
and never looked into my eyes.
I've got news for you, lady:
There's more money in lampshades
than arty degrees.
She left the next morning without a goodbye,
now Stanley will tell me I don't even try. (*He sniffs disgustedly*)
The house reeks of perfume!

Stanley I'd hoped they'd get on,
but Dimitri and Mother had nothing in common.
I'm used to his habit
of helping himself
from a communal dish
with his personal spoon.
Mother however, is hot on good manners.
She delivered a lecture
involving utensils, in general terms.
Dimwit yawned in her face,
with his mouth full of pasta
and burped at the end of the meal.
(*Wistfully, as if towards his departing mother*)
So elegant though,

	in her pale cashmere throw.
Dimitri	Mutton dressed as Yves St Laurent. (*He makes a good-riddance gesture, as if briskly blowing dust from the palm of his hand. Then he sits forward, inviting the audience to come closer*)
	Stanley was mugged by a freezer repair man, tied to the bed and relieved of his Rolex.
	I came home to find him in pain and hysterics.
	I called a young doctor, a gay rights supporter, he treated Stan's rope burn
	and gave him sedation.
	I don't think he'll risk
	any further flirtation.
Stanley	When we heard it was filmed on Dimitri's island, we rushed to see *Shirley Valentine*
	Dim fancied Tom Conti,
	but I felt for Shirley
	who was, as she said,
	"looking for adventure, when the time for adventure has passed." (*He sighs heavily, and eats a biscuit without much pleasure*)
Dimitri	We don't get asked out very often,
	now that we don't entertain.
	But I was never at ease with Stanley's friends
	and he wasn't at ease with mine.
Stanley	We used to give wonderful parties:
	Parties designed round a theme.
	Balinese, for example,
	with guests in grass skirts.
	They'd arrive after dark, I hasten to mention, since I'm talking of all-male affairs.
	Complaints about bongos. The police paid a visit and stayed for a drink, with their eyes out on stalks.
Dimitri	So. These days we keep to ourselves.

We can't get enough of our house, and our garden,
not to mention the cats, the fish and the bonsais…
We decorate every few years.
So far: art deco, Victorian, Regency,
Japanese, fifties—

Stanley —and a nightmare in stripped pine and shantung!

Dimitri glares at him

We're currently changing to "French Country House"
Inspired by the great Terence Conran—

Dimitri —a man who has no taste in lighting.
Stanley Bit of a shock at the showroom.
Lunch with the manager. Widespread reshuffle.
I'm to move sideways, to imports and exports,
not a demotion, he says.
"Old hands must move over, make way for the New Wave,
bearing in mind that the shoppers we're after,
are twenty to thirty, with money to burn."

Pause

Jean-Paul will replace me, he has the right image.

Dimitri Stanley was so hurt he couldn't discuss it.
They're edging him out,
but he can't bear to face it. They're losing a treasure,
well, stuff them, who needs them?
The demand for my lampshades has never been greater.
But Stanley is cut to the quick.

Stanley takes a bite of a biscuit

The Stanley Parkers

	He put on four pounds in a week.
Stanley	We just have to face it:
	Dimwit and I are a middle-aged couple.
	He's had his eyes done, and looks a lot younger.
	(*He again uses the biscuit tin lid as a mirror, peers into it, and pushes up an eyebrow with his finger*)
	I might do the same.
	People we know are beginning to die.
	Heart attacks, strokes, they're dropping like flies.
	I'm into a diet with far less cholesterol.
	I haven't changed shape—
	but my fat feels much lighter
Dimitri	Soon after Stan lost his job,
	he had an affair with a po-faced young hairdresser.
	Hardly a week in it, not from the heart.
	I just let it pass.
	Well, I know why he did it,
	his ego was bruised and in need of a boost.
	A five-minute wonder
	and not from the heart. (*He shrugs philosophically*)
Stanley	If Dimitri found out
	he would never forgive me,
	but I had a wee fling
	with a Byronesque hairdresser.
	He was here just a week for a highlighting course.
	A boost to my battered old ego.
Dimitri	We are Derby and Joan, worse than any straight couple
	and proud to announce that we're Godparents now!
	Well, two Godfathers then, if you want to split hairs.
	An old friend of Stanley's
	bestowed this great honour.

We couldn't stop smiling all day. (*He looks at Stanley with love*)

Stanley nods and smiles sheepishly

Stanley Graffiti appeared on the wall of our garden:
"Two geriatric perverts live here"
Is that how folks see us?
I'm upset, I'll be honest.
Geriatric indeed. Bloody cheek!

Pause

                When I think what we spent on our eyes.

Dimitri Sometimes, when things run smoothly,
I long for a little… catastrophe.
a blight on the roses…
a flood, or an earthquake,
just some little thing.
And later I'm sorry for having such thoughts,
because somehow I know
that the best times are now.

Pause

Stanley I'd just had a shave
when I noticed the swellings,
the glands in my neck
twice their usual size.
"DIMITRI!" I called, and he came in and felt them.
His face became ashen,
his fingers were trembling.
"Let's not get excited," he said, very calmly.

> But he said it in Greek. (*He puts the biscuit tin aside*)

Dimitri stops working on the lampshade

Dimitri We don't understand why it's happened to us,
to Stanley, my poor, harmless Stanley.
At the clinic,
I watched through a glass panelled door,
as the doctor explained
what the future might hold.
And Stanley… (*his voice breaks*)
… my baby … (*he recovers his voice*)
backed into a corner,
and wouldn't stop talking,
not wanting to hear.

Stanley The doctor, a boy with a serious face,
is anxious to contact my fling.
And Dim must be told and his memory jogged,
in case he can add anything.

Dimitri After six months, I'm clear,
to the clinic's surprise.
But Stanley has full-blown, with all that implies.

He offers Stanley a biscuit. Stanley declines. Dimitri closes the tin, and places it at the end of the bed

> We've vowed to tell no-one.
> We'll say it's lymphoma.
> The doc says the progress is somewhat the same.

Long pause, then softly:

Stanley Anger…

Dimitri   Denial…
Stanley   Bargaining…
Dimitri   Depression…

They turn to look at each other

Stanley \
Dimitri } (*together*) Acceptance.

Stanley (*quite briskly*) I hate to leave Dimwit, he's not very bright.
   Knows nothing of mortgage rates,
   taxes and rebates.
   He'll be ripped off by lawyers and all kinds of tradesmen.
   He won't ask for discounts—
   says all that's for peasants,
   stuck-up little sod!

Pause. (If the actor wears glasses they should now be removed)

   I wish now we'd more friends,
   but it's too late for parties.
Dimitri (*cheerfully*) I told Stan a joke:

He kneels on the bed and helps Stanley take off his kimono. Stanley is tired but not too weak at this stage. While Dimitri removes the kimono, Stanley removes the pillow from under his pyjamas and slides it down the bed, out of sight

   There's an old queen waiting for a doctor's diagnosis.
   "I'm sorry to tell you," the doctor says gently,
   "but your symptoms are related to Aids."
   "What did you say?" cries the patient in horror.

"Aids." says the doctor.
"Thank God," says the patient, "for a moment I thought you said AGE!"

Stanley and Dimitri laugh until they find themselves crying. Each turns away, hoping the other won't notice. They rapidly pull themselves together. Dimitri folds the kimono with great care and places it on top of the biscuit tin at the end of the bed. (If Stanley has worn spectacles, they can now be added to the pile, creating a little shrine)

Stanley (*with diminished energy*) I've discovered a lesion.
Kaposi's Sarcoma. (*He touches his chest*)
Left to itself, it will burrow like a rodent
through the wall of my chest.
With treatment, it will burrow more slowly.
The trick is to hide it from Dim.

Dimitri Stan has four lesions, one front and three back.
He imagines they're hidden from me.
He was angry this morning, when I tried to kiss him.
Amazing, his strength when he pushed me away.
We can still share a bedroom,
but all holds are barred. (*He resumes work on a lampshade*)

Stanley (*with angry strength*) Dim won't understand that some things have to change,
that some types of contact could kill him.
It's hard to accept,
because some days I'm well.

Pause

He works on his lampshades
right here in the bedroom,

        and tries not to leave me alone.
Dimitri (*stitching away cheerfully*) I'm gradually setting up
        house in the bedroom,
        so Stanley need never feel lonely.
        No hospice for him—not while I can take breath.
        He's better off here, in our beautiful home.

Stanley smiles and slides down in the bed until he is lying fairly flat, apart from his head

Stanley   In the old days, whenever Dimitri got shirty,
              I used to hum Zorba, just softly hum Zorba,
              to hint at his humble beginnings.
              (*Distantly*) Life with him has been … so good.
Dimitri   No. Not many visitors, all in all.
              Our mothers have been and gone.
              I invited our Godchild, he failed to arrive,
              so I gather the word is out.

The lighting changes, casting shadows on the two characters and creating a less rosy ambience

Stanley (*absolutely still, but speaking normally*) No pain. Just
                incredible weakness…
              To butter my toast is a marathon task,
              to chew it, an Olympian feat.
              But Dimitri persists.
              He feeds me and shaves me and ferries a bedpan.
              Whistling and singing while he rushes around.
              He never relaxes.
              I think he imagines
              that as long as he keeps moving,
              I will. (*He closes his eyes*)

Dimitri   He sleeps a lot now and he's wasting away,
there's a faraway look in his eyes.
He's quiet and sometimes he can't seem to hear—
but it's still my old Stanley in there.
His ex-manager came, brought us Turkish delight.
Held a scarf to his face,
said he didn't want to pass on his flu!
Stanley dozed through the visit—
at least that's what I thought,
till he winked at me suddenly,
and out of the blue—

Stanley, eyes still closed, holds up his middle finger. Dimitri does it with him, beaming gleefully. Stanley manages a smile

gave Mr El-Bosso the finger!

Now Stanley becomes very still, his eyes closed. Dimitri looks at him, then smoothes the bedclothes around him, tidies the collar of his pyjamas, removes an imaginary hair from the pillow

After a pause, he reaches out his hand as if to touch Stanley's head, then stops himself. Then he tentatively lays his left hand on Stanley's right shoulder. Stanley doesn't waken and Dimitri is content with this small contact

After a moment, Stanley slowly moves his left hand to cover Dimitri's. He opens his eyes and they look at each other and smile

Stanley   (*barely audibly*) Thank you. (*After a pause, Stanley removes his hand*)

Dimitri rises from the bed, goes to the hi-fi, and lowers the stylus onto a record

We hear some very authentic Greek music; a lament, perhaps sung by a choir, and slow at the beginning

Dimitri takes a large white handkerchief from his pocket and twists it around his hand, leaving its tail trailing from his closed fist

He begins to dance, his arms outstretched, his bowed head following the movements of his feet

Stanley, smiling, inclines his head, the better to see

Dimitri dances, not moving much at first, then travelling across the stage. He swoops and rises skilfully, with absolute concentration

The music grows faster and Dimitri begins to turn on the spot, dancing faster and faster, his head thrown back, his arms high, his hands outstretched

Slow fade to Black-out

CURTAIN

FURNITURE AND PROPERTY LIST

On stage: Spacious double bed
Small collection of lampshades, some newly made and
    wrapped in polythene
Stacked hi-fi system
Greek albums
Dimitri's leather slippers
2 ostentatious bedside lamps
Stitching needle
Lampshade
Biscuit tin. *In it:* biscuits

Personal: **Stanley:** pregnancy-style pillow, spectacles (optional)
Dimitri: handkerchief

LIGHTING PLOT

Property fittings required: two lamps
Interior setting throughout

To open: Warm and cosy lighting

Cue 1   **Dimitri**: "…so I gather the word is out."   (Page 16)
            Cast shadows on the characters;
              less rosy ambience

Cue 2   **Dimitri** dances faster and faster   (Page 18)
            Slowly fade to black-out

EFFECTS PLOT

Cue 1   **Dimitri** lowers the stylus on to a record   (Page 17)
Authentic Greek music

Printed by
The Kingfisher Press, London NW10 6UR